I0481284

CRYPTOCURRENCY INVESTING

The Ultimate Guide About Top Cryptocurrencies for Investing and Perfect Strategies to Make Money

By Sam Sutton

~~~

TABLE OF CONTENTS

INTRODUCTION

Congratulations on downloading this book and thank you for doing so.

The following chapters will teach you everything that you need to know about investing in cryptocurrencies. They will provide you with the right knowledge that will allow you to join the cryptocurrency race, turn the odds in your favor, and dominate the cryptocurrency market. This is your chance to rake in serious and continuous profits.

Chapter 1 talks about the myths that surround the cryptocurrency market and reveals the main rules orfacts behind them.

Chapter 2 discusses the basic rules that you need to know when you invest in cryptocurrency.

Chapter 3 talks about mining cryptocurrency and how the mining process works.

Chapter 4 explains the blockchain technology, which is the backbone technology of bitcoin and other cryptocurrencies.

Chapter 5 explains the different kinds of cryptocurrency wallets, as well as how to securely store your bitcoin or any other cryptocurrency.

Chapter 6 talks about the top 10 cryptocurrencies in the market and where you can track them.

Chapter 7 discusses the most popular cryptocurrency exchanges that you can use to buy, sell, or trade cryptocurrencies.

Chapter 8 reveals powerful and effective investment strategies that you can use to turn the odds in your favour and significantly increase your chances of making high and continuous profits.

May this book be your guiding light to success and financial freedom.

There are plenty of books on this subject on the market, thanks again for choosing this one! Every effort was made to ensure it is full of as much useful information as possible. Please enjoy!

CHAPTER 1:

MYTHS ABOUT CRYPTOCURRENCY MARKET AND MAIN RULES OF THE MARKET

There are myths that surround the cryptocurrency market. As an investor, it is important for you to know the truth behind the myths in order for you to have the right view and understanding of the cryptocurrency market. Let us uncover the facts behind these popular myths one by one:

» *Myth #1: Cryptocurrencies are a big bubble that is about to burst.*

For years, many people have viewed bitcoin and other cryptocurrencies as a mere bubble that is about to burst. Because of this fear, which arises from an erroneous perception, they fail to take advantage of the cryptocurrency market, while those who have the will to take risks and believe in cryptocurrencies have been able to earn a high amount of profit. In fact, some of them have even made their way to complete financial freedom simply by investing in cryptocurrencies like bitcoin, Ethereum, and others. Still, even today, there are those who say that cryptocurrencies are just a bubble. Well, it is up to you if you are going to believe those who claim that it is a bubble. However, the fact remains that while other people think that cryptocurrencies are a mere bubble, there are those who take the risks and believe in the power and value that cryptocurrencies offer, and they are able to rake in serious profits. Whether a bubble or not, it is true that investing in cryptocurrencies can be a very lucrative investment.

The main rule of the market dictates that a cryptocurrency will only "burst" if it has no value or loses its value. But there is no "bubble" to talk about it. This is because bitcoin offers real value to the market. It is widely recognized as a cryptocurrency that can be used for trading.

» Myth #2: Unlike the U.S. dollar, cryptocurrencies have no real value.

Years ago, the value of the U.S. dollar was pegged to the value or price of gold. However, the dollar was soon weaned off of gold. The result was that the dollar did not have anything to back itself except the faith of the people in its value. The same applies when you use cryptocurrencies. It is the faith of the people that a certain cryptocurrency has a value that allows it to continue to have value and importance in the market. Also, it is noteworthy that many cryptocurrencies these days do not just function as mere substitute for money. In fact, they offer something that makes them even more valuable. For example, the altcoin Ethereum promotes the use of smart contracts and distributed applications on its blockchain. Another example is Ripple, which actually helps banks to have quicker transactions at a lower cost. So, as far as value is concerned, it can easily be said that cryptocurrencies, especially those that are in the mainstream, are highly valuable.

» Myth #3: Cryptocurrencies are for criminals.

Due to the anonymity enjoyed by cryptocurrency users, there are people who think that cryptocurrencies are primarily created and used for illegal activities like money laundering. However, this is not true. Although cryptocurrency users enjoy a high level of anonymity, they still do not have complete anonymity. This is why those who abused the use of cryptocurrencies to commit illegal acts have already been arrested. Also, if you look at the facts, those who buy guns and other weapon often use fiat money (the official currency of a state) and not cryptocurrencies. Fiat money has been used in illegal activities for many years. This happens even today, especially in the black market.

» *Myth #4: Investing in cryptocurrencies will only make you lose your investment in the long run.*

Just like any other investment, there are risks involved when you invest in any cryptocurrency. Hence, it is true that you might lose your investment, just as you can also easily lose your investment when you put your money in the stock market, especially if you do not know the ins and outs of the market. In any kind of investment, there are those who make a nice profit and there are also those who lose a part of or even their whole investment. Nonetheless, when you invest in cryptocurrencies, you may or may not lose your investment. In fact, there are so many cryptocurrency investors who have earned a very high amount of profit. Remember the classic example: Had you invested even just $400 in bitcoins back in 2009 or 2010, then you would have earned millions in profit by now. There are many real-life success stories of people who have earned millions in profit. In fact, there are many cryptocurrency investors who have earned their way to financial freedom.

» *Myth #5: Investing in cryptocurrencies is a fast and easy way to make money.*

Now, there are also those who think that investing in cryptocurrency is a quick and easy way that leads to financial freedom. However, the truth is that even though there are people who have earned millions of dollars and attained financial freedom by simply investing in cryptocurrencies, they are not an everyday occurrence. Many professional and successful traders spend hours on a daily basis just studying the highly volatile cryptocurrency market, and they are very careful whenever they enter or leave a position. Most successful cryptocurrency traders are highly meticulous to details and are very careful with their investment decisions. If you are serious about having continuous success and profit in the cryptocurrency market, then it is a basic rule that you should do hours of research and analysis. Keep in mind that you are dealing with a quickly evolving and highly competitive market

» Myth #6: The blockchain can easily be hacked.

Here is the truth: Nobody has ever successfully hacked the blockchain. You may read reports of various cryptocurrency wallets being hacked, but those do not refer to the blockchain network itself. The blockchain is a highly secure system and network that is spread over a vast number of computers. Of course, an attack against the blockchain is possible; however, for an attack against the blockchain to be successful, then the attack must possess at least 51% of the hash power of the entire blockchain network. Needless to say, since blockchain is spread over a vast network of computers, obtaining the said 51% is virtually impossible.

Another bit of good news is that cryptocurrency wallets have already upgraded their security features. In fact, these days, you could barely hear any news of any cryptocurrency being hacked, especially if the person observes certain protective measures, such as using a strong password and enabling two-factor authentication, among others. If you still worry about the security of your cryptocurrency wallet, then you can always use a cold wallet to completely protect it from hackers, malware, and viruses.

» Myth #7: Governments will prohibit the use of cryptocurrencies.

The general rule is that the use of cryptocurrencies is legal. If you look at the facts, it is easy to see that almost all governments allow the use of cryptocurrencies in their respective jurisdictions. Over time, more and more states become open to the idea of finally using and embracing cryptocurrencies. A good example of this is Russia, which used to outlaw the use of cryptocurrencies in its territory. In 2017, Russia legalized the use of bitcoins and other cryptocurrencies. Although China closed down all of its local cryptocurrency exchanges, it was for the purpose of preparing some regulations on the use of cryptocurrencies, not for the purpose of permanently isolating itself from the cryptocurrency market. Singapore declared that it would not yet impose any regulation on the use of cryptocurrencies. In many countries, like in the U.S., Canada, Europe, India, Philippines, and many others, the use of bitcoins and other cryptocurrencies is legal. In fact, cryptocurrencies are only prohibited in a very few countries, such as in Ecuador, Bolivia, and Kyrgyzstan, and few others.

Some say that the people behind these cryptocurrencies will soon be arrested. It should be noted that cryptocurrencies like bitcoin are decentralized. This means that there is no person, organization, or authority that exercises control over it. The system works on its own. Hence, there is no one that can be arrested or be put on trial.

» *Myth #8: It is hard to understand the cryptocurrency market.*

Of course, if you read the white paper of a cryptocurrency, you will most likely find it hard to understand because of the technical terms that are used. But cryptocurrencies are easy to understand as long as you are willing to learn and engage in research. For example, by the time that you finish reading this book alone, you will already be equipped with the right knowledge of what cryptocurrencies are about, as well as how you can make an investment and earn a nice profit. In fact, investing in stocks is much more technical than understanding and investing in cryptocurrencies. If you can devote several hours and if you are truly willing to learn, then you can rest assured that you will be able to understand the ins and outs of cryptocurrencies in no time.

So, there you have it. These are the popular myths that surround the cryptocurrency market. Now that you know the truth behind the myths, it is time for you to know the basic principles that govern these cryptocurrencies, so that you will have a much better understanding of what cryptocurrencies really are.

CHAPTER 2:

BASIC PRINCIPLES OF CRYPTOCURRENCY

What is a *Cryptocurrency?*

A *cryptocurrency* is a type of digital asset. It has no physical existence. Instead, it is stored and held electronically (online). It is "crypto" because it is secured using *cryptography,*which refers to the practice of converting information into codes in order to ensure secure communication. Cryptography was used during the Second World War when it was extremely important for the army to ensure that their communications and correspondences were protected against enemy spies. It is a "currency" in the sense that it functions as a substitute for money. Hence, you can use it to buy certain products and services from merchants who accept cryptocurrencies, such as Microsoft, Steam, Peach Airlines, Virgin Galactic, Fiverr, and Overstock, among many others. To date, there are over a thousand different cryptocurrencies in the market, and the number keeps on increasing.

Cryptocurrency vs. Fiat money

Although a cryptocurrency like bitcoin may be used as a medium of exchange, it is still not considered as *fiat money*. What is fiat money? Fiat money refers to the official currency of a state, which is regulated by its government. An excellent example of fiat money is the U.S. dollar. This is because a cryptocurrency is decentralized, which means that there is no person or group that exercises authority over it. This makes it free from all forms of manipulation and undue advantage. Since cryptocurrency is not considered fiat money, it is also not considered *legal tender*. Legal tender refers to that which a "debtor may compel a creditor to accept payment." Of course, the exception to this is if payment in cryptocurrency is agreed upon by the parties in their contract.

It is noteworthy that although a cryptocurrency is neither fiat money nor legal tender, it is still widely accepted by numerous businesses and individuals around the world. In fact, over time, the number of cryptocurrency users has been constantly increasing. Indeed, so many people these days are very eager to learn and understand how to use (and invest) in cryptocurrency.

Bitcoin vs. Altcoins

Bitcoin is the number one cryptocurrency in the world. Back in 2008, a paper was published on a cryptography mailing list. The paper was entitled *Bitcoin: A Peer-to-Peer Electronic Cash System* under the name Satoshi Nakamoto. The following year, bitcoin was finally launched in the market. Back then, bitcoin did not have any substantial value. In fact, just like all other cryptocurrencies (altcoins), it was the cryptocurrency community members themselves who decided the value of bitcoin. There was even a transaction where two pizzas delivered by Papa John's were bought for 10,000 bitcoins. You can still see how this transaction took place on the *bitcointalk* forum, and you will also see other comments that obviously reflect that the people did not take bitcoin seriously at that time. Today, bitcoin is the most successful and highly-priced cryptocurrency in the world. As of January 18, 2018, the price of 1 bitcoin is around $11,600 USD.

To date, there are more than 1,000 different cryptocurrencies in the market. Still, bitcoin is recognized as the number one and most successful cryptocurrency in the world. In fact, it has so strongly established itself that it is now considered as the leading standard of all cryptocurrencies to the point that all other cryptocurrencies are merely called as *altcoins*, which is short for *alternative coins*.

However, it is noteworthy that investing in altcoins can also be a highly lucrative investment. For example, in 2017, the altcoin known as OmisgeGO increased by more than 1,200% in price in just several weeks. Also in 2017, the altcoin, Ethereum, which is the second most successful cryptocurrency in the market and is currently the next in rank to bitcoin, increased by over 13,000%.

Anonymity

Cryptocurrency users enjoy a high level of anonymity. In a transaction, the name and other personal details of the parties involved remain private. Instead of revealing personal details, only the cryptocurrency wallet address, amount involved, and the time stamp are usually the things that are shown to the public. Hence, if privacy is a concern, you will definitely find using cryptocurrencies very helpful.In fact, some cryptocurrencies like Zcash and Dash will allow you to almost completely hide or make private your transaction.

How a cryptocurrency transaction works

A cryptocurrency transaction may not always work the same way, depending on how its blockchain system is structured. However, the usual cryptocurrency transaction, such as when you use bitcoins, has three main parts:

✓ Input

Before anyone can send any cryptocurrency to another, it is only logical that he must first have enough cryptocurrency to send in his cryptocurrency wallet. This means that he must first receive cryptocurrency from another. This is what is referred to as an *input*. Once you have an input, then you can start sending or using cryptocurrency.

✓ Output

The output refers to the recipient's cryptocurrency wallet address. Take note that a single cryptocurrency wallet can generate multiple different addresses. The *output* refers to the wallet address of the recipient that will receive the cryptocurrency that you will send.

✓ Amount

The *amount*, of course, refers to the amount involved in a transaction; therefore, if you are going to send 1 bitcoin, then the *amount* involved in the transaction is 1 bitcoin.

Additional notes

When you are the one who is sending cryptocurrency to another, be sure that you get the right cryptocurrency wallet address. Every cryptocurrency wallet address is unique from the others. It looks like a string of randomly-generated letters and numbers. Once a transaction is confirmed, there is no way that you can cancel or change it, so make sure that you send the cryptocurrency to the correct wallet address. Sending cryptocurrency is fast and easy, especially if you are using a hot wallet. If you are using a cold wallet, then this might take a longer time. The different types of cryptocurrency wallets will be discussed later in the book.If you are the recipient (receiver), then all that you need to do is to give your cryptocurrency wallet address to the sender and wait for him to send you cryptocurrency.

Why Invest in Cryptocurrency?

It is true that although a cryptocurrency functions as a substitute for money, the majority of cryptocurrency holders do not use it as a medium of exchange. Instead, they buy and sell cryptocurrency as a form of investment. Is it lucrative enough? Well, just remember the classic example: Had you invested even just $400 in bitcoin back in 2009 or early 2010, then you would have earned multimillion dollars in profit by now. Needless to say, bitcoin is not the only cryptocurrency in the market that is worth investing in. There are also many altcoins in the market whose price surge as high as 2,000% (and even way higher) in just a short span of time. So, is it profitable to invest in cryptocurrency? The answer is a resounding *yes*. However, just like any other investment, there are also risks involved when you invest in cryptocurrency, and this includes the risk of losing your whole investment. This is the reason why professional and successful cryptocurrency investors use strategies. When you use effective and powerful strategies, you can significantly increase your chances of making the right investment decision. Do not worry; these strategies are also revealed in this book. So, just keep on reading and learning, and you will soon gain a strong foundation to be able to dominate the cryptocurrency market and use it to your advantage. One thing is certain: If you are serious about making continuous profit by investing in a cryptocurrency or different types of cryptocurrencies, then you should be willing to spend hours in research. Just like anything that is worth pursuing, success in the cryptocurrency market requires time, efforts, practice, and hard work.

High volatility

The cryptocurrency market is known for having high volatility. What is *high volatility*? It means that the price of a cryptocurrency usually rises and falls rapidly and significantly. This allows its price to fluctuate and increase by more than 50% (or higher) in 24 hours. Of course, the opposite is also true, which means that its price can drop quickly. This is why you need to study and analyze the market, so that you will be more able to predict the price direction that a particular cryptocurrency will take. Indeed, the cryptocurrency market has a very high volatility. In fact, this is the reason why some investors are afraid to invest in ay cryptocurrency since a market with a high volatility also involves a high risk. However, if you come to think about it, it is not really something that you should be discouraged of. You have to realize that it is exactly the high volatile nature of the cryptocurrency market that makes it a very lucrative investment. It is exactly why you could profit by more than 20,000% in a short span of time. Although there are risks involved, as can be expected of any worthy investment, there are strategies that you can use to turn the odds in your favor and significantly increase your chances of making a highly profitable investment.

CHAPTER 3:

MINING CRYPTOCURRENCY AND HOW THE MINING PROCESS WORKS

Let us discuss another interesting topic in the world of cryptocurrency known as *mining*. Mining is another investment option that you have when you deal with cryptocurrencies. So, what is *mining*? Mining refers to the process of verifying and adding transactions or blocks on the blockchain. The blockchain is the central technology of bitcoin and other cryptocurrencies. It is composed of a record of transactions known as *blocks*. There is a constant demand for miners because without the miners, no new record or block can be added to the blockchain. This means that no transaction can be completed. Hence, mining is a very important activity.

How Does It Work?

Before any new record is added to the blockchain, it must first undergo a process of confirmation and verification. This is what mining is all about. The first thing that a miner does is to verify whether or not a certain transaction is valid or not. Next, a miner will bundle the recent transactions into a block. After that, the miner selects the header of the latest block and connects it to the new block as a hash. The next step is the most difficult part, and that is to solve the Proof of Work (PoW). This is where a miner solves a difficult mathematical puzzle. Once the miner is able to find a solution to the puzzle, only then will the block be added to the blockchain. Hence, this is the time when a transaction will be fully completed. Miners are compensated usually in the form of a transaction fee every time they are able to mine a block. This is the usual way that mining works. Of course, depending on how the system of a certain cryptocurrency is structured, the mining procedure may have some differences.

How to Mine Cryptocurrency

There are several ways to mine cryptocurrency. Let us discuss them one by one:

✓ Computer Mining

You can use your computer to mine cryptocurrency. This is also known as CPU mining, since you will be mining using the power of your computer's CPU. This is a good way to experience what it feels like to actually mine cryptocurrency. You simply have to download the software, and then you can use your computer to start mining. There are free mining software options that you can download online. A popular mining software that you can use is the GUIMiner. It should be noted that you cannot expect to earn a decent amount of cryptocurrency if you only mine using your computer alone. The reason is that a computer does not have sufficient mining power to mine blocks quickly. You will most probably end up with more electricity expenses than the total amount of cryptocurrency that you can mine. Hence, only consider computer mining as way to partake of the actual mining experience, but do not expect to earn any profit from it. Also, when you use computer mining, you should be cautious of overheating problems. You should pay attention to this since too much overheating may break your computer. Be sure to give enough time for your computer to cool down.

✓ Hardware Mining

Since a computer alone does not generate enough mining power to earn you a decent amount of cryptocurrency, the better approach is to do hardware mining. Hardware mining makes use of hardware in order to increase your mining hash power. There are various mining hardware options that you can find online. You might want to check Amazon and eBay. Take note that even if you use hardware, you will still have to use your computer. Hence, you should still be careful with overheating issues. Be sure to give your computer and your hardware enough time to cool down. A major drawback of using this mining approach is that good-quality mining hardware can be expensive, and it will take time before you can fully recover your expenses and break even. In choosing your mining hardware, you should pay attention to the mining power and the electricity consumption. Figure out the necessary computation to see how much you will most likely earn. It is not uncommon to find a bit of strong mining hardware that also spends much electric power. And it is worth repeating that you should pay attention to any overheating issues.

✓ **Cloud Mining**

Cloud mining is probably the most popular and recommended method of mining cryptocurrency these days. When you use cloud mining, you will no longer have to worry about purchasing any hardware or any overheating issue. You do not even have to use your computer. In fact, you do not even have to mine cryptocurrency. All that you need to do is to relax and wait for your mining company to send to you your cryptocurrency, which is usually on a weekly basis or as soon as you reach the minimum threshold amount. Okay, this seems too good to be true. So, what is the catch? The catch is that before a cloud mining company begins to mine for you, you must first make an investment (pay the cloud mining company). A typical offer may look like this: Invest 0.5 bitcoins and receive 0.008 bitcoins every week. At first glance, this seems like a really good deal. You just need to do a simple computation, and you will be able to tell when you will recover your investment, and then the profits that you can earn. However, the problem here is that the offer is usually just the *expected* return and does not refer to the actual return that you will receive. Therefore, there is the possibility that you might receive less than the agreed amount. In our given example, it could be less than 0.008 bitcoins every week. Not to mention, there have been reports where investors did not receive any payment or profit from their cloud mining company. Therefore, be careful since there are many scammers out there. It is important that you only work with a trustworthy and reliable mining company. Before you invest or make any form of deposit, be sure to check the latest ratings and reviews given to the cloud mining company.

It is also not uncommon for cloud mining companies to fix an expiration date to the contract. Hence, you should be able to get back your investment and also make a good amount of profit before the contracts expires. Once the contract expires, then the cloud mining company will no longer mine for you. In order to renew the contract, you will have to pay the mining company again. It is noteworthy that some cloud mining companies may allow you to have a lifetime contract with them. Just be sure to check the terms and conditions of the contract. As can be expected, those that offer a lifetime contract will most likely be the ones that will offer a low return. Regardless of the duration of the mining contract, make sure to read and understand all of the provisions in the contract. This is also a good time for you to hire a good lawyer to make sure that the contract is fair and reasonable before you make any investment, especially if you intend to make a big investment.

Although mining cryptocurrency can still be a highly profitable activity, many experts advise that if you want a better way to earn cryptocurrency and without any limitation to the profit that you can earn, then you should learn investing directly on cryptocurrencies instead of mining them. There are different investing strategies that you can use to increase your chances of making a high amount of profit, as revealed in this book.

CHAPTER 4:

BLOCKCHAIN
TECHNOLOGY

Blockchain technology, or simply known as *blockchain*, is the backbone technology of bitcoin and other cryptocurrencies. The first decentralized and public blockchain was developed by Satoshi Nakamoto, the man behind the number one cryptocurrency of all, bitcoin. Bitcoin, as well as other cryptocurrencies, uses the blockchain technology. So, what exactly is this blockchain technology? Blockchain is a public, decentralized, and distributed ledger. Hence, it functions as a repository of all transactions. It also has a very high level of security.

A blockchain is composed of records known as blocks. Every new block that is added to the blockchain must first be verified and pass through a series of confirmations. This is to ensure that the record that is being added is legitimate and genuine. Once a record is added to the blockchain, it can no longer be removed, altered, or withdrawn. Every new block that is added is connected to the previous block using what is known as a hash pointer. This makes all the records or blocks on the blockchain to be interconnected with one another. No part of the blockchain can be amended, changed, removed, or in any way be modified, unless there is a concurrence of at least a majority (51%) of the users in the network. Take note that the blockchain is connected to a vast network of computers. As a distributed ledger, any changes or additions made to any of the records will be reflected to all other users. Hence, if a certain record is added, then such record will be distributed to all the other users in the network, and so they will also be informed about it.

The blockchain is public in the sense that all transactions are viewable and verifiable to everyone. Do not worry; as we have already discussed, all of your personal information remains confidential. The blockchain is also known for being decentralized, which means that there is no central authority or organization that exercises control over it. Therefore, you can rest assured that it is free from any and all forms of bias, manipulation, undue control, and advantage.

As we have already discussed, blockchain technology is highly secure. For an attack against the blockchain to be successful, it must possess at least 51% of the total hash rate of the entire network. Since the blockchain is spread over a vast computer network, obtaining the said 51% is virtually impossible.

Today, blockchain is gaining popularity of its own apart from it being associated with the use of cryptocurrencies. This is because blockchain technology can also be applied to things other than cryptocurrencies and financial-related matters. In fact, those who people who may not like cryptocurrencies are very much interested in exploring possible opportunities of using blockchain technology.

CHAPTER 5:

WALLETS AND HOW TO SECURELY STORE BITCOIN

Why do you need a bitcoin wallet? Well, before you can start using and investing in bitcoins, you first need to have a place where you can store bitcoins. The place where you keep or store your bitcoins is what is known as a bitcoin wallet. There are different kinds of bitcoin wallets that you can use. You should understand their differences so that you will know just which wallet type will best suit your needs. Here are the different types of bitcoin wallets:

» *Web Wallet*

A web wallet is also known as an *online wallet*. This is the most commonly used type of bitcoin hot wallet in the world. Good examples of a bitcoin web wallet are Coinbase, GreenAddress, and Exodus. A web wallet is very convenient to use. You simply have to connect to the Internet to manage your wallet account. Although there have been security issues with web wallets in the past, it is noteworthy that many web wallets have already upgraded their security features, which makes the possibility of being hacked extremely difficult, if not impossible. It is also very easy to make a web wallet. You simply have to sign up for an account with a wallet provider. The whole signing up process only takes less than three minutes to complete.

» *Mobile Wallet*

A bitcoin mobile wallet is another type of hot wallet. As the name implies, it is the kind of bitcoin wallet that you can download on your mobile phone. Many web wallets also function as a mobile wallet. Normally, you can download the mobile wallet as an application from the Apple and/or GooglePlay store. These days, it is very easy and convenient to just use your phone to access the Internet. A mobile wallet will allow you to manage your account, send and receive bitcoins, and even buy and sell bitcoins, simply by using your mobile device.

» *Desktop Wallet*

A bitcoin desktop wallet is a type of cold wallet. Hence, it has a greater security than the aforementioned hot wallets. When you use a desktop wallet, you will store your bitcoins in a computer. The computer does not necessarily have to be a desktop computer. A laptop computer will also work just fine. Keep in mind that unlike a hot wallet, a cold wallet is not exposed to the hazards of the Internet. Therefore, when you use a desktop wallet, you should not connect the computer to the Internet anymore in order to keep it secure and protected.

» *Hardware Wallet*

A hardware wallet is another type of bitcoin cold wallet. It is also like a desktop wallet, but instead of keeping your public and private keys in a computer, you store them in some form of hardware, such as a USB. There are now specialized wallets being sold in the market precisely for this purpose. One of the most popular and highly recommended hardware wallets is the *Ledger Nano*. Just like when using a desktop wallet, you should avoid connecting your hardware wallet to a computer that is connected to the Internet or a computer that is affected by a virus or any kind of malware. This is an important preventive measure to keep your hardware wallet safe and secure. Again, when it comes to using a cold wallet, the main priority is the security of your wallet account.

» *Paper Wallet*

A paper wallet is where you store and print your public and private keys on paper. This is a very popular kind of cold wallet. It is suggested that you print several copies just in case you lose a copy. Needless to say, you should store them in a safe place. It is also common for paper wallet to have a QR code that you will need to scan before you can access your account and transfer funds. Simply put, you need to be in possession of the paper wallet in order to gain full access to your bitcoin wallet account

Which Wallet Type Should You Use?

When deciding which type of bitcoin wallet to use, you have to consider how you intend to use bitcoins. If you intend to make regular transactions, then you should use a hot wallet. Most hot wallets are available on the web as well as on mobile; hence, as far as convenience is concerned, you can rest assured that you will not have a problem with it. However, if you just want to make a long-term investment in bitcoin and if you are concerned about the security of your wallet, then you can use a cold wallet. Of course, you are not limited to using just a single wallet. Hence, if you want, you can use both kinds of bitcoin wallets, depending on your needs and how you intend to use bitcoins. You can also use multiple hot wallets at the same time. As the saying goes, "Do not put all your eggs in one basket." The same advice applies when it comes to storing your bitcoins.

Tips to Securely Store your Bitcoins

Regardless of whether you are using a hot or cold wallet, the security of your bitcoin wallet remains of high importance. Here are the best practices that you should observe in order to keep your bitcoin wallet safe and secure:

• *Use a strong password.*

Be sure to use a strong password. A strong password should combine lower and uppercase letters. You should also use numbers and symbols. Needless to say, it should not be something that other people can guess correctly. Therefore, do not use your birthday or your alias as a password. It is also advised that you use a long password of at least 15 characters long. From time to time, you should also update (change) your password.

• *Request a new bitcoin wallet address.*

Most bitcoin wallets will allow you to request a new bitcoin wallet address at any time and as many times as you want. Do not worry; this is very easy to do and you do not have to pay anything. You can do this with just a few clicks of a mouse and in less than 10 seconds. Take note that a single bitcoin wallet can generate many different wallet addresses. It is the wallet address that is used when sending and receiving bitcoins. It is a good practice to request a new bitcoin wallet address for every new transaction that you make. This is an effective way to minimize the exposure of a certain bitcoin wallet address, which is a good preventive measure that can minimize your risk. Again, make it a habit to request and use a new bitcoin wallet address every time that you make a transaction.

• *Check if the page is secure.*

Before you input any sensitive information, like your account password, on a website, you should first see to it that the page is secure. This is easy to do. Simply look at the URL bar and you should see a green padlock and/or the word "Secure" somewhere on the side of the URL bar. This signifies that the page is secure and that it is safe to key in sensitive information. Keep in mind that you should never enter your password or any other sensitive information if you are not sure if the page is secure.

• *Avoid public Wi-Fi connections.*

These days, it is very easy to connect to public Wi-Fi, especially when you are not at home. Although it is okay to use public Wi-Fi, especially if you are just browsing websites, it is not recommended that you access your bitcoin wallet over a public connection. The reason is because there are hackers out there who take advantage of public Wi-Fi connections and use them to pry into other users connected to the public Wi-Fi. A public Wi-Fi is mostly unsecure by nature, so you should not use it if you are going to input any sensitive information or when accessing/managing your bitcoin wallet.

Some notes when using a cold wallet

When you are using a cold wallet, you should make sure that the cold wallet is of good quality. Keep in mind that although a cold wallet can protect you against hackers and all other related Internet risks, it cannot protect you from the risk of having your wallet stolen or broken. Hence, be sure that it is in a good working condition and keep it in a safe place.

(It is noteworthy that these practices are also as effective when you are storing altcoins.)

CHAPTER 6:

TOP 10 CRYPTOCURRENCIES AND WHERE TO TRACK THEM

To date, there are more than 1,000 cryptocurrencies in the market, but only a handful of them are able to draw enough market attention to establish a real value. Let us look at the top 10 cryptocurrencies in the market:

✓ Bitcoin (BTC)

Of course, the first one on the list should be *bitcoin*. Bitcoin is the leading standard when it comes to cryptocurrencies. Indeed, it is the most successful cryptocurrency in the world. As of January 19, 2018, the price of 1 bitcoin is around $11,572 USD.

✓ Ethereum (ETH)

Ethereum is considered by many as the second most successful cryptocurrency in the world. There are even some people who strongly believe that Ethereum will be able to overtake bitcoin and be the number one cryptocurrency in 2018. However, many experts say that this is far from happening, as bitcoin remains very strong in the market. Ethereum promotes the use of smart contracts and distributed applications on its blockchain. Ethereum is the platform, while its cryptocurrency token is known as *ether*. As of January 19, 2018, the price of 1 ether is around $1,058.

✓ **Ripple (XRP)**

Unlike most cryptocurrencies that seem to antagonize banks as if to take their place, Ripple actually helps banks. Ripple was launched in 2012, and it "enables banks to settle cross-border payments in real time, with end-to-end transparency, and at lower costs." Also, unlike other cryptocurrencies, Ripple is structured in such a way that it does not need mining. As of January 19, 2018, the price of Ripple is around $1.64 USD.

Zcash (ZEC)

Zcash was introduced in the market in 2016. It is based on a decentralized and open-source system. Zcash defines itself as follows: "If Bitcoin is like http for money, Zcash is https." Zcash gives primary importance to privacy. It allows the use of selective transparency. This selective transparency allows its users to enjoy a high level of privacy by hiding the details as to the sender, recipient, and even the amount involved in a transaction. This is referred to as a "shielded transaction." As of January 19, 2018, the price of 1 Zcash is around $501.

✓ **Dash (DASH)**

Dash used to be known in the market as Darkcoin. Dash is structured in such a way that its transactions can be made to be almost untraceable. It was introduced in the market in 2014, and it was able to quickly establish a name for itself. Although its name changed from Darkcoin into Dash, its features remain the same. The term, Dash, is short for Digital Cash. As of January 19, 2018, the price of Dash is around $849.

✓ **Litecoin (LTE)**

Litecoin was released in 2011. Hence, it is not a new cryptocurrency player in the market. It is one of the early competitors of bitcoin. If bitcoin was considered gold, then Litecoin wanted to be the silver version. Its features closely resemble those of bitcoin.

However, Litecoin has a faster block generation than bitcoin, and this means that it can confirm and complete transactions much faster than bitcoin. As Proof of Work (PoW), Litecoin uses what is known as "scrypt." As of January 19, 2018, the price of LTE is around $196.

✓ Monero (XMR)

Monero was made out of the donations coming from the cryptocurrency community. It was introduced in the market in 2014. Its main focus is on decentralization and scalability. It promotes the use of ring signatures. When you use ring signatures, a legitimate transaction gets mixed up with a set of false transactions. This is an effective way to "hide" or make your transactions private since people will not be able to identify the legitimate transactions from those that are false, especially that the false transactions will also appear and look as if they were valid. AS of January 19, 2018, the price of XMR is around $337.

✓ Lisk (LSK)

Lisk is quite a new cryptocurrency. It was introduced in the market in 2016. It functions like Ethereum in the sense that it allows the use of applications on its blockchain. When you use Lisk, you can create your blockchain on top of the Lisk blockchain. As of January 19, 2018, the price of Lisk is around $23.

OmiseGO (OMG)

OmiseGO was launched in 2017, which makes it a fairly new cryptocurrency. It aims to provide a simplified and more effective financial service. Its slogan is "Unbank the Banked." It is one of the altcoins in the market that is based on Ethereum blockchain. In 2017, the price of OMG increased by more than 1,200% in just a few weeks. As of January 19, 2018, the price of OMG is around $17 USD.

✓ NEO (NEO)

NEO is known as China's largest cryptocurrency. It was launched in 2014 under the name *Antshares*, but it was renamed later on to NEO by its developers. NEO is also the name by which this cryptocurrency is commonly known. People also call it as China's Ethereum. It functions just like Ethereum. NEO is China's first and number one coin. NEO has also seen a significant increase in price in recent months. As of January 19, 2018, the price of NEO is around $145.

Additional Notes:

The prices of these cryptocurrencies fluctuate continuously. You can easily track their prices by visiting the following sites:

https://coinmarketcap.com/
https://www.coingecko.com/en

CHAPTER 7:

MOST POPULAR CRYPTOCURRENCY EXCHANGES

If you do a search online, you will find many different cryptocurrency exchanges. As an investor, it is important that you work with a trustworthy and reliable exchange platform. Let us look at the most popular cryptocurrency exchanges:

✓ Coinbase

Coinbase has millions of investors and customers in the world. It is probably the most popular exchange platform in the world. Coinbase makes it very easy to buy and sell selected cryptocurrencies. Coinbase currently offers only three cryptocurrencies: Bitcoin, Ether, and Litecoin. Coinbase has an excellent reputation and is trusted by many professional investors.

✓ Kraken

Kraken started in 2011. It offers many types of cryptocurrencies, including Ripple, Monero, ICONOMI, and other altcoins. It does not just allow you to buy and sell cryptocurrencies, but you can also trade bitcoins with fiat money, such as the U.S. dollar, Japanese Yen, and others.

✓ Cex.io

Cex.io also provides different cryptocurrencies to choose from. Just like Kraken, it also allows you to trade cryptocurrencies with fiat money. It also offers a cold storage. It also provides a simple way to buy bitcoins at a price that is close to the actual market rate.

This is excellent for traders and investors who are just starting out.

✓ Poloniex

Poloniex offers many cryptocurrency choices. It was launched in 2014, and is now one of the most popular cryptocurrency exchanges. Its trading environment looks professional and secure with more than 100 cryptocurrency pairs to choose from. It has a high trading volume. It is also fast and easy to create an account with Poloniex. You would not have a hard time with it even if you are a complete beginner. It also imposes a low fee for trading.

✓ Shapeshift

Shiftshift is one of those rare platforms where you do not even have to sign up for an account. You can trade directly using a direct and straightforward approach. It does not provide any policy for fiat money, but only offers the exchange between and among different cryptocurrencies. This is simplest and fastest way to convert one cryptocurrency into another.

✓ Bitstamp

Bitstamp is not a new platform. In fact, it has been in the market since 2011, and it is trusted by many cryptocurrency investors. It provides its users with high security features, such as two-factor authentication and multi-signature technology. Its customer support is also available round the clock. Indeed, it has earned a good reputation in the cryptocurrency community.

✓ Binance

Binance is another famous cryptocurrency exchange platform. It also has an excellent mobile application. Although it may not offer a professionally designed platform, you can be sure that trading with Binance makes the process really simple and easy. There are also various cryptocurrencies to choose from. The site is easy to use, and it is also recommended by many serious cryptocurrency investors.

✓ Bitfinex

This is considered as one of the largest cryptocurrency exchange in the market. Although it is trusted and used by many investors, Bitfinex already got hacked which resulted to the loss of around $72,000,000 worth of bitcoins. It has also faced several technical issues. Still, many cryptocurrency investors are happy and satisfied with Bitfinex.

CHAPTER 8:

INVESTMENT
STRATEGIES

I f you want to have continuous success in the cryptocurrency market, you need to apply effective and powerful strategies that can turn the odds in your favor and increase your chances of making a profit. Here are notable strategies that you should learn and practice:

» *Fundamental Analysis*

As they say, "Knowledge is power." When you use fundamental analysis, you need to have knowledge of the fundamentals or the basics. The key to using this strategy is to have as much knowledge and understanding of the cryptocurrency market, as well as the cryptocurrency that you intend to invest in. When you do fundamental analysis, you should make it a habit to be updated on the latest news, especially those that are closely related to the cryptocurrency market, such as news about the economy, market competition, market acceptance, technological developments, and related government regulations, among others. You need to gain as much information as possible. It is a basic rule in investing that the more that you understand the market, the more likely that you can come up with a profitable investment decision.

If you are serious about making money by investing in cryptocurrencies, then it is considered a must that you learn and use this strategy. To give you an idea: When Russia legalized the use of bitcoins in its jurisdiction, the price of bitcoin and other cryptocurrencies increased. However, when China declared that it would shut down its local exchanges, the price of bitcoin and many other altcoins dropped significantly. When it was featured on the news that the co-founder of bitcoin sold all his bitcoins and invested in bitcoin cash (an offshoot of bitcoin), the price of bitcoin fell and the price of bitcoin cash increased. As you can see, by simply gaining basic information and doing your analysis, you can have a good idea on how certain cryptocurrencies will respond in the market. Once you can predict how certain cryptocurrencies will most likely move in the market, you can then take appropriate actions to take advantage of the market and make a profit.

This strategy can be applied even if you are using a different strategy. In fact, this is so important that it has also been referred to as the lifeblood of investment. Whether investing in cryptocurrencies, stocks, bonds, or real estate, you will definitely find this strategy very helpful.

» *Technical Analysis*

If you are more of a visual person, then you will probably enjoy doing technical analysis. When you use this approach, you will have to study charts and graphs that show the price movements (past and present trends) of a cryptocurrency. The concept behind technical analysis is that all the many factors that influence a cryptocurrency have their final effect upon the price. Hence, by simply analyzing the price movements of a cryptocurrency, you also get to deal with all the many elements that affect it. In a way, this is like a simplified version of fundamental analysis.

When you use technical analysis, you need to learn how to read and identify patterns. Yes, patterns do exist from time to time. However, take note that they often come and go. Therefore, do not expect to always see a pattern or trend every time that you look at a certain chart or graph. A common mistake is to force yourself to see a pattern even if there is nothing at all to be seen. You need to keep an open mind. However, once you recognize a certain pattern, then you should be ready to take advantage of it.

Just like fundamental analysis, you can combine technical analysis with another strategy. In fact, many cryptocurrency investors combine both fundamental and technical analysis. According to experts, mastery of fundamental and technical analysis can increase your chances of success by more than 75%.

» *Averaging Down*

This is a good way to earn a high amount of profit. However, this is also an aggressive approach so you need to be cautious when you use it. The best way to explain this strategy is by using an example: Let us assume that you want to invest in bitcoin and that the price of bitcoin is $9,000. If the price of bitcoin increases, then you make an easy profit. However, if the price drops, for example, down to $8,700, then you should make a buy order at the said lower amount. Now, if it decreases again, say, down to $8,300, then you should make another buy order, and so on and so forth. Simply put, you just have to keep buying the cryptocurrency concerned while its price keeps on falling. Now, although this may seem like you are investing in a losing asset, the truth here is that you are actually making a profitable investment. The key to profit here is when the price of the cryptocurrency (in this case, bitcoin) involved recovers either back to its original value (its price when you first applied this strategy), or higher. When this happens, all the buy positions that you have made will experience a nice profit.

This strategy is also a good way to take advantage of the volatility of the market, especially when the prices of cryptocurrencies constantly rise and fall. Although this strategy may seem very practical and profitable, it is noteworthy that it is also highly aggressive, so you need to be careful with it.

» *Buy and hold*

This is probably the most basic strategy that you can use. However, it is worth noting that there are people who have earned millions of profit simply by using this strategy. So, how does it work? As the name implies, it involves buying a particular cryptocurrency and then holding on to it. You should hold on to it as you wait for its price to increase. Once its price increases over time, you can then sell it at a profit. How profitable is this strategy? Well, just imagine having invested in bitcoin four years ago using this strategy, then you would have made a very high profit by now. Although this strategy is often used for a long-term investment, you can also use this strategy for a short-term investment.

Before you apply this strategy, it is important for you to first study the cryptocurrency market. You need to identify the cryptocurrency that is most likely going to increase in price. You cannot just use this strategy at random. You also need to make sure that you are investing in a valuable and profitable cryptocurrency.

» *Altcoin Spread Out*

These days, many investors like to invest in altcoins. The reason is that altcoins, especially the new ones, have such a big room for improvement. In fact, it is not uncommon to find altcoins that increase their value by more than 200% in just a short period of time. When you use this strategy, you should divide your total capital into parts. There is no hard and fast rule as to how you should divide your capital, but it is suggested that you divide it into at least four equal parts. This will give you four chances or investments. If you divide it into four, then it means that you will invest in four altcoins. The key is to invest in a valuable altcoin whose price will most likely increase significantly. Pay attention to new and start-up altcoins in the market as they have a big room for growth and improvement. It is normal for start-up altcoins to increase even as high as 1,000% over time. Hence, even if you divide your capital into four and only one of those four investments turns out to be profitable, there is a good chance that you will still end up in positive profit.There are three points to consider when choosing a strong altcoin: value, effective promotion, and market acceptance. Make sure that you invest in an altcoin that has a good value. It should also be effectively promoted by its developers and its followers/supporters. Last but not least, it should attract the attention and interest of the market.

CONCLUSION

Thanks for making it through to the end of this book. We hope it was informative and able to provide you with all of the tools you need to achieve your goals whatever they may be.

The next step is to apply everything that you have learned and start earning continuous profits. It is time for you to put your knowledge into actual practice. *Now* is the perfect time for you to make a difference and change your life for the better.

Finally, if you found this book useful in anyway, a review on Amazon is always appreciated!